CONTENTS

PROGRAMME OVERVIEW

The CAAPS Programme comprises 30 x 40 minute lessons from which it is recommended you select just 24, ie. 6 for each year group.

- Year 3 Unit comprises 7 lessons

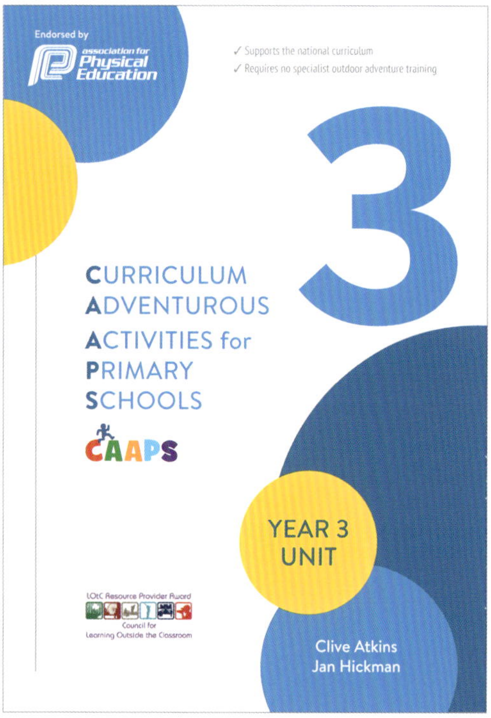

- Year 4 Unit comprises 7 lessons

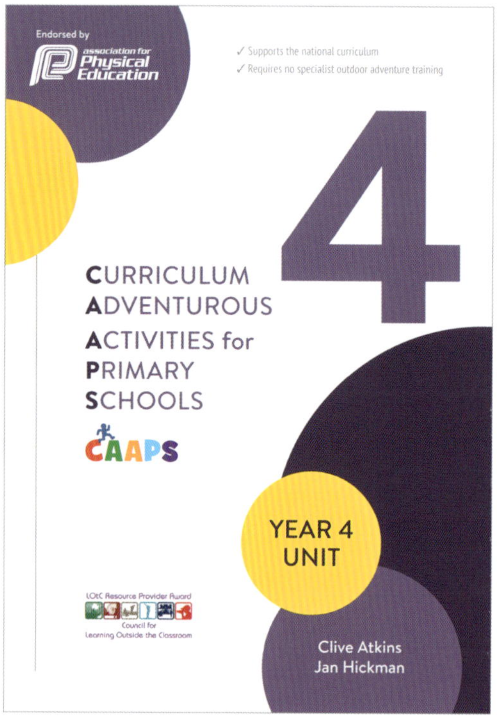

- Year 5 Unit comprises 8 lessons

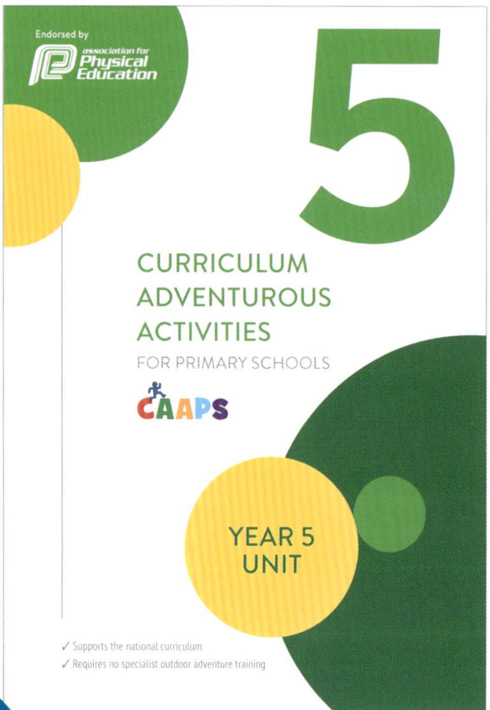

- Year 6 Unit comprises 8 lessons

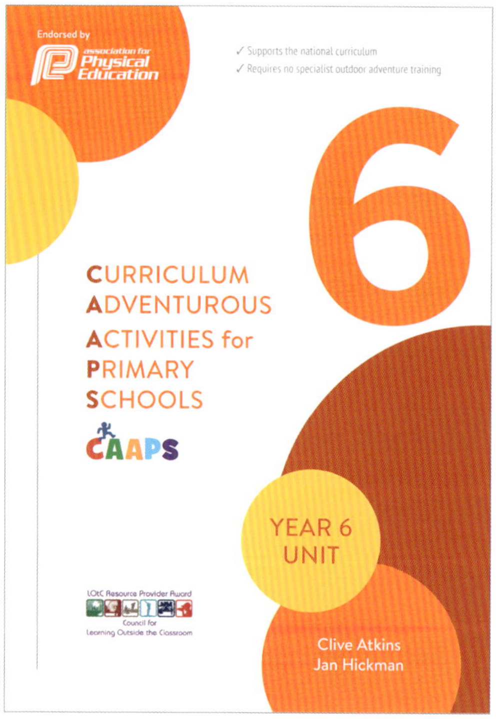

PROGRAMME OVERVIEW

OVERVIEW OF THE CAAPS PROGRAMME

The CAAPS Programme meets the Department for Education (DfE) 2014 national curriculum requirements for physical education: Key Stage 2 (KS2) – Outdoor and Adventurous Activities (OAA):

> *'Pupils should be taught to take part in outdoor and adventurous activity challenges both individually and within a team.'*

The Programme has been designed by Clive Atkins (Outdoor Education Adviser) and Jan Hickman (Physical Education Adviser) for KS2 colleagues who may have limited physical education expertise and be unable to attend a training course.

The CAAPS lessons generally follow a logical sequence in terms of difficulty but the activities are interchangeable. **Lessons do not need to be delivered in the order listed.** Furthermore, the activities themselves are not rigid, and you are encouraged to experiment by varying the activities according to the group, environment and resources available. Normal physical education safety procedures apply when delivering the activities, and where there may be specific safety issues these are highlighted in the appropriate lesson sections.

All the activities have been pitched at an 'average' level for each year group. However, differentiation is possible, and activities can be easily adapted to suit the needs of individual pupils or groups. Each lesson gives an overview and should be regarded simply as an 'aide-memoire'. If you are unfamiliar with the activities, refer to any associated resource materials for organisation, differentiation and developmental ideas. As well as catering for individual challenge and competition, significant emphasis is placed on team working, leadership and other personal and social skills, which can be readily transferable to other aspects of physical education. Learners will also have the opportunity to increase their speed, strength, agility and fitness, and improve their awareness of the importance of a healthy lifestyle.

Remember that **enjoyment** is a key factor in maximising learning potential, and always consider this element when planning and reviewing lessons.

In order to protect pupils, your staff and your school, and keep up-to-date on the latest developments in Physical Education, we recommend that schools should become members of the Association for Physical Education (afPE) www.afpe.org.uk

ASSESSMENT

The Physical Education National Curriculum (2014) sets out the aims, purpose of study and content for physical education. It does not specify a detailed overview of the nature and content of learning. However, it does present attainment targets that pupils should reach by the end of each key stage. The CAAPS programme has been devised with the KS2 attainment target at the forefront:

> *'Pupils should continue to implement and develop a broader range of skills, learning how to use them in different ways and to link them to make actions and sequences of movement. They should enjoy communicating, collaborating and competing with each other. They should develop an understanding of how to succeed in different activities and sports and learn how to evaluate and recognise their own success'.*

CAAPS is an aspirational programme that has incorporated the above attainment target throughout the Units. If used well, and adapted to meet the needs of pupils in individual schools, then accurate and meaningful assessment can take place.

It is statutory that at KS2 the Physical Education programme curriculum should teach pupils to take part in outdoor and adventurous activity (OAA) challenges both individually and within a team. The CAAPS programme has been written to support schools in the delivery of this aspect. High quality OAA planning and delivery that meets the needs of all pupils, will enable them to learn, apply and understand the skills and processes applicable to this programme of study and support them in reaching the attainment target.

Assessment is integral to planning, teaching and learning and the primary purpose of assessment is to measure pupil attainment and progress against standards. The removal of 'levels' has enabled schools to introduce their own approaches to formative assessment in order to support pupil attainment and progression. The statements on page 7 of each CAAPS Unit (taken from the QCA OAA scheme of work, archived on the EVOLVE National Library www.national-library.info), may be used used as a device for matching performance of individual pupils against these national expectations. These statements are embedded throughout the CAAPS programme. Appropriate assessment methods, that will improve learning in OAA, include peer observation, videoing and analysing performance and using learner statements. These methods can be integrated into the CAAPS activities to assess pupils' knowledge, skills and understanding. Assessment information recorded in this way can also be kept as sampled evidence and will be helpful in moderating teachers' judgements.

YEARS 3 AND 4 EXPECTATIONS

Some children will be able to:

- follow simple marked trails in familiar environments and, with help, identify where they are on the trails
- help others to solve problems they have been set, taking an active part in the work
- follow others' suggestions
- know that they need to be careful so that they are safe
- recognise when they have been energetic
- describe what they did when following a trail or solving a problem
- comment on how well activities were completed.

Most children will be able to:

- use maps and plans to orientate themselves and travel around a simple course
- respond when the task or environment changes and the challenge increases
- plan sensible responses to physical challenges or problems
- work increasingly cooperatively with others, discussing how to follow plans and solve problems
- recognise that different tasks make their bodies work in different ways
- comment on how they went about tackling tasks, and respond to feedback on how to go about their work differently.

Some children may even be able to:

- use more detailed plans and diagrams that take them from familiar to less familiar areas (eg from hall to playground)
- find their way and recognise where they are on a plan or diagram
- solve problems using a range of approaches
- use ideas they have learned in one problem or task to help them solve another
- work and behave safely when working on their own and in small groups
- show initiative when working in a group
- explain why different activities make their bodies work in different ways
- identify ways to prepare physically for the activities
- identify strengths and weaknesses in the way challenges are approached
- suggest alternative solutions.

RESOURCES

Each CAAPS unit resource is self-contained and comprises all the lesson plans, additional information, photocopiable resources and details of other resource materials required.

An overview of the main resources required for this unit is given on Page 10, with full details given in each activity description. Please note that orienteering activities use terms such as control cards, markers and clippers/punches. Examples of these appear on the next page.

Maps of the school site are also required. Sketched maps are perfectly adequate in the early stages. These can easily be reproduced directly from Google Earth or Google Maps (subject to copyright). Alternatively, as a lesson in its own right, pupils could make their own maps of the area in pairs, and then vote on whose would be the best to use for activities. Ideally however, we recommend that schools invest in a professionally produced orienteering map of their site, in both pdf and editable formats. Many companies provide this service.

For efficiency, and to help ensure that the programme is fully integrated into the PE curriculum, it is recommended that schools keep each lesson's resources in their own labelled box (see example below).

SOME EXAMPLES OF CONTROL MARKERS

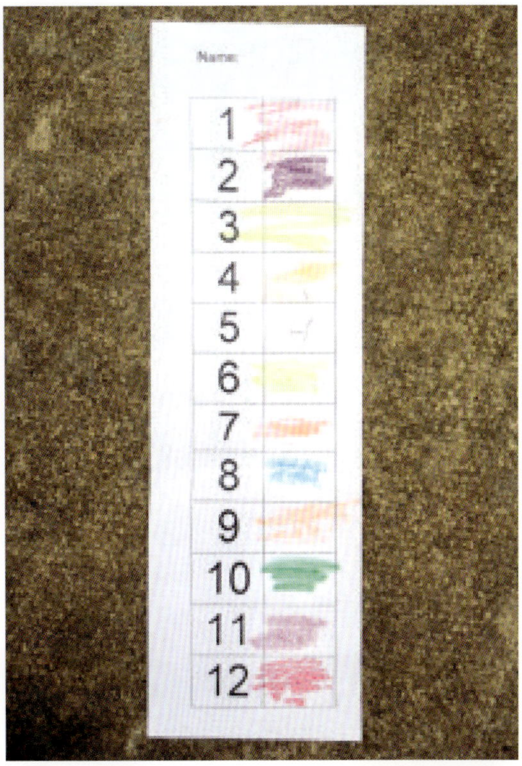

PROGRAMME OVERVIEW

Activities in blue = hall/gym   Activities in green = outside

Choose six lessons from:

LESSON	ACTIVITY	OVERVIEW	MAIN RESOURCES REQUIRED
LESSON 1	Human Letters	Making letter shapes with body	None
LESSON 2	First Map	Very basic map orientation	• Photocopied 'maps' from resources – one per pair • 1 gym bench • 2 gym mats • Circle of cones or rope • One pencil per pair
LESSON 3	Memory Trail	Following a trail and remembering objects	• String, cord or rope (50 metres) • 20 assorted random objects • Clipboards/paper/pencils
LESSON 4	Map Symbol Race	Relay race matching names to symbols	• Photocopied sets of map symbols and names
LESSON 5	Clipping Control Cards	Running to 20 markers	• Up to 20 orienteering clippers/ punches (or can improvise) • Photocopied control cards
LESSON 6	Follow The String	Following a trail around school grounds	• String (at least 300 metres) • Maps of school grounds with course showing (optional) • 10 hanging letters (see description) • Blank paper • Pencil stubs/crayons
LESSON 7	Rolling Ball	Transporting a tennis ball using plastic guttering	Per pair: • One tennis ball • One section of plastic guttering (approximately 60-100cms)

LESSON 1 – HUMAN LETTERS

www.caaps.org.uk

ACTIVITY:
Spelling out letters using only the human body

LEARNING OBJECTIVE:
To be able to respond to a problem set

ORGANISATION AND RESOURCES:
Hall or Gym. No resources required

YEAR 3

LESSON 1 – HUMAN LETTERS

LESSON PHASE	LEARNING ACTIVITY	PLANNED QUESTIONS
Starter activity (Warm-up)	• In pairs, walk around the hall/gym and check that it is safe. • Discuss what a hazard is. • Is there anything here that is not a hazard to you, but might be a hazard to younger children? • Walk in and out of each other in a designated area. • On the command '1', circle your arms x2, on '2', bend and touch the floor, and on '3' star jump x2. • Carry on walking after each action has been performed, and listen for the next command. • Do the above '1, 2, 3 Command' game but add jogging in between the actions.	How do we know we have been energetic? What is happening to our body as we exercise?
Developing skills and their application through Human Letters	• Find a space in the hall. • Your teacher will call out a letter of the alphabet and you will try to make the letter using only your body. • Repeat but with a partner. • Try the same activity in groups of 3/4/5 • In a group of six, make up a word. • Differentiate as appropriate. **Particularly useful letters** • Individually: I, T, X. • In pairs: A, H. • In 3s: N, M. • In 4–5s: O, Q, S.	Did you find a good way to form the letters? How could you improve your letter shapes? Are there other ways to try?
Additional ideas	• Split the class into 2. Each group forms a much longer word, eg 'teamwork' on the opposite side of the playground. The other group guesses it. • The whole class could make a phrase or sentence. • Ask the Headteacher to identify the words/sentence. Please feed back comments and additional ideas at www.caaps.org.uk	
Review and assess (Cool-down)	Look at images you could capture on a camera during the session. Can they identify the word?	Share your favourite letter with the rest of the group. Did you feel part of the group in today's lesson? How are these feelings linked to health?

Learning Outcomes:
Least able: Will help their partner and group in solving the problems set.
Majority: Will respond to the problems set creatively, with a partner and in a small group.
Most able: Will show leadership skills in solving the problems set.

Teacher's notes to inform future planning:

Teacher's notes to inform future planning:

LESSON 2 – FIRST MAP

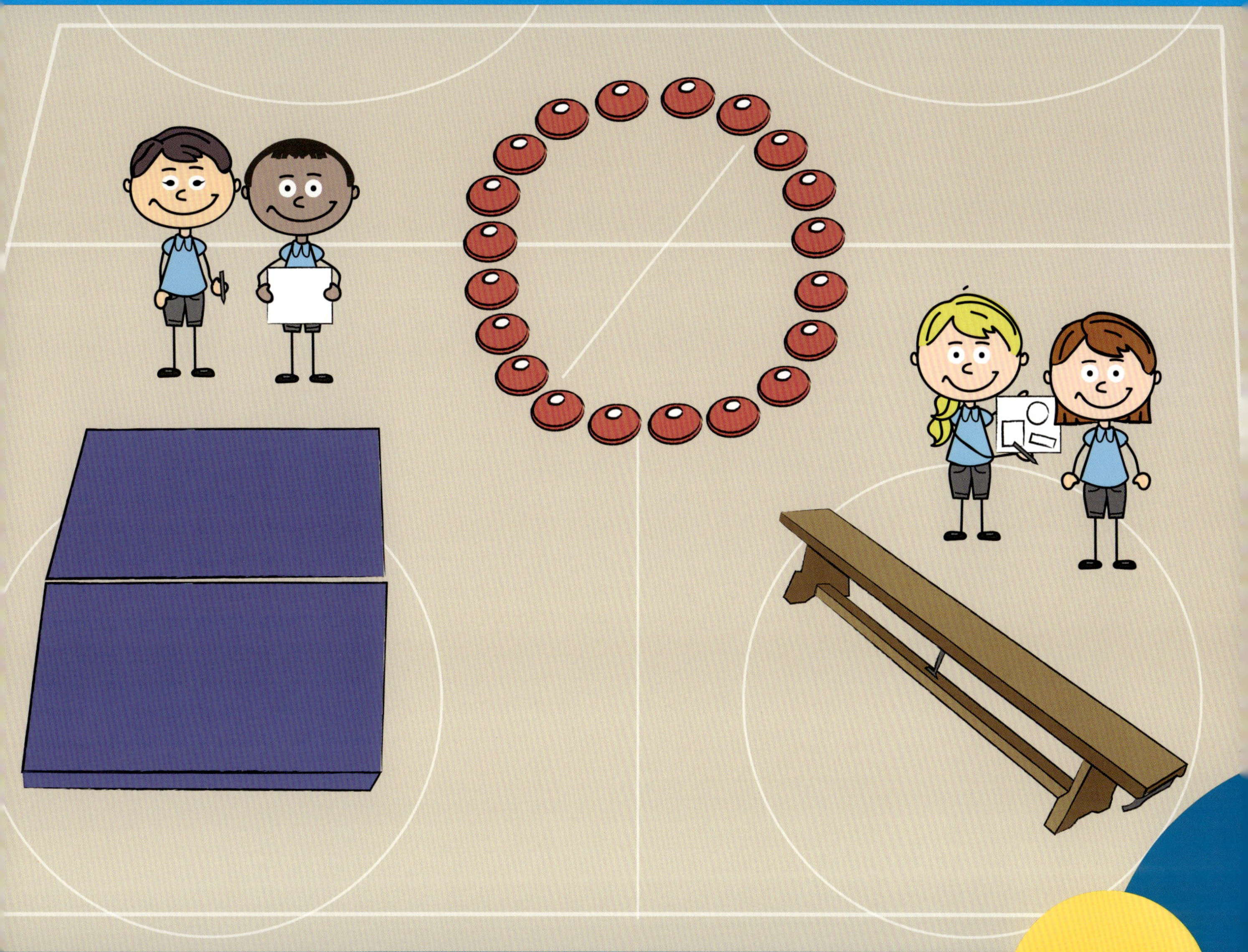

ACTIVITY:
Basic map reading

LEARNING OBJECTIVE:
To be able to read a basic map and orientate the body and map accordingly

ORGANISATION AND RESOURCES:
To set out the course: 1 gym bench, 2 gym mats (ideally to form a square), about 20 cones to form a circle. 1 pencil and photocopied map per pair (see template)

YEAR 3

LESSON 2 – FIRST MAP

LESSON PHASE	LEARNING ACTIVITY	PLANNED QUESTIONS
Starter activity (Warm-up)	• Walk around the hall/gym. Is it safe? Are there any hazards? • Jog in and out of each other, taking care to swerve to develop agility while moving. • Gradually increase the speed of the jog lifting knees higher and faster, or jog slowly. • Alternatively, if jogging is too difficult, try walking. • Emphasise that it is NOT running round the hall but moving in and out of each other at random. • 'Leave your footprints everywhere, go to the middle of the area, the sides, the corners, changing speed as you move.'	Can you change your speed as you jog? Are you able to increase your speed and still avoid each other? Who is able to maintain a fast speed and swerve, avoiding others?
Developing skills and their application through First Map	• Sit around the outside of the hall in pairs. • One 'map' per person (see template). Put the map on the floor and set it (turn) so that it matches what you see. • Point on the map to where you are. • In pairs, move to another place. Set the map on the floor and point to where you are. • Teacher walks around the area while pupils follow with finger on map. • One person in the pair runs to a place in the area and their partner points to where they are on the map. • Put 2 sticks in an arrow head shape on the floor, pupils draw this on map. • One partner sits facing away from the area and closes eyes. Partner tears corner off map, writes initials on, folds and puts this somewhere in the area. Returns and marks spot on the map. Partner studies the map then runs to retrieve it. • Differentiate as appropriate.	Did you always set the map correctly? Were you able to identify where your partner was on the map? Were you able to find the piece of paper straight away or did you have to search for it?
Additional ideas	• Use larger colour maps, with same colours as objects, eg blue square for blue mats. • One person in the pair draws a route from they are sitting, around 2 objects and back. Add direction arrow, and half way point X. Partner follows route and stops at X. Teacher checks, then continue. • Introduce compass points (e.g. sit on East side of square). Please feed back comments and additional ideas at www.caaps.org.uk	
Review and assess (Cool-down)	Ask the pupils: • To walk very quickly, gradually getting slower and slower; and stop. • To follow the route on the map as the teacher walks around.	What was your favourite thing about the session?

Learning Outcomes:
Least able: Will follow their partner and describe what they did when following a trail.
Majority: Will be able to identify where they are in relation to the map.
Most Able: Will be able to follow more complex trails without aid, help others and recognise exactly where they are on the map at all times.

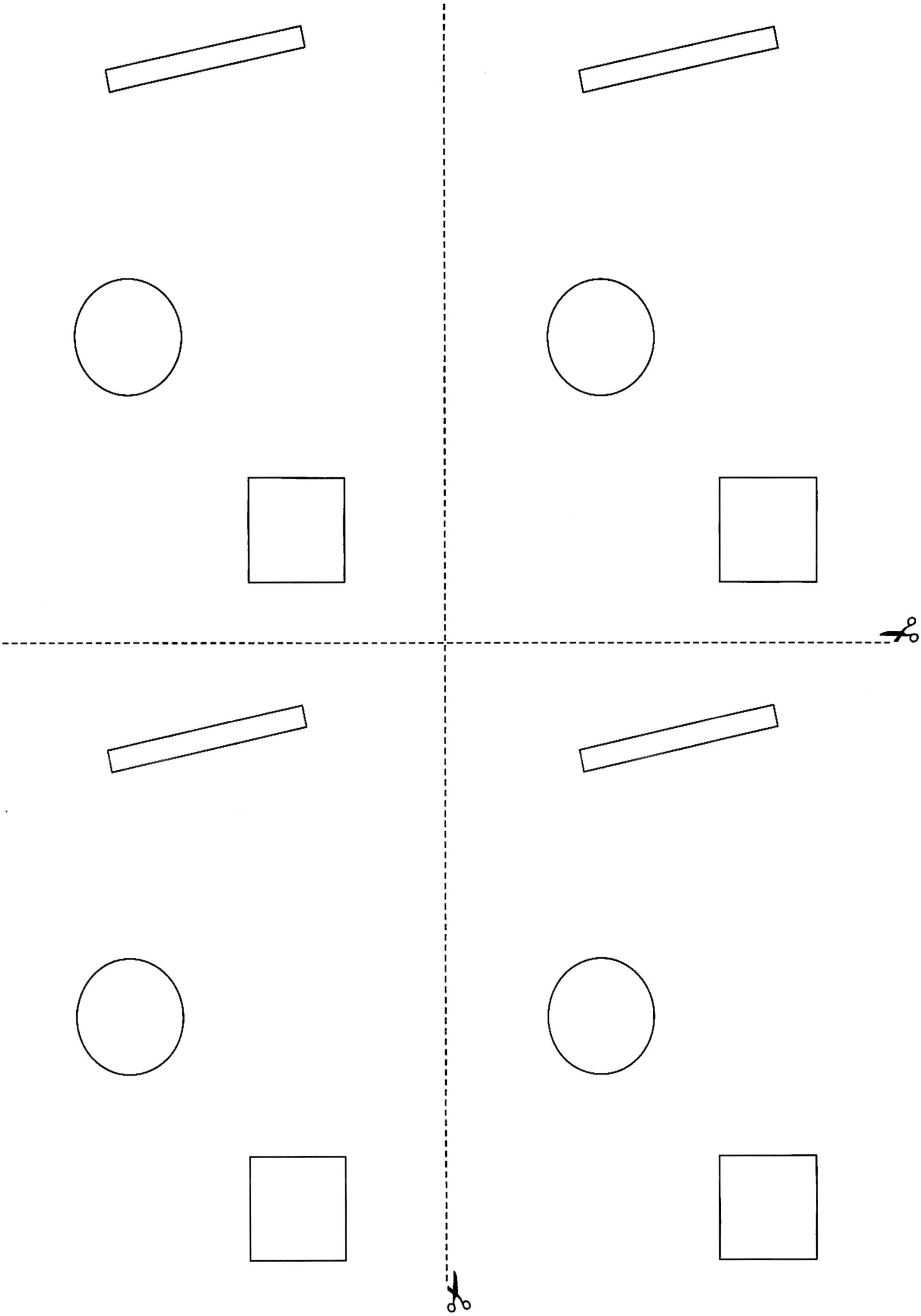

Teacher's notes to inform future planning:

LESSON 3 – MEMORY TRAIL

ACTIVITY:
Following a marked trail and remembering as many items as possible along the way

LEARNING OBJECTIVE:
To devise a simple plan and follow a marked trail

ORGANISATION AND RESOURCES:
50-100m string or cord. 20 random objects (see description). Blank paper and 1 pencil per group of 4-6. Note: the start and finish areas need to be out of sight of the objects

LESSON 3 – MEMORY TRAIL

LESSON PHASE	LEARNING ACTIVITY	PLANNED QUESTIONS
Starter activity (Warm-up)	• Jog in and out of each other in a designated area (netball court, - or make it smaller, try one third of the netball court!). Take care to swerve to avoid each other and develop agility as you move. • Gradually increase the speed of the jog, lifting knees high and using the arms. • Alternatively, try walking if jogging and avoiding others is too difficult. (Emphasise that it is NOT running round the area, but moving in and out of each other, using all of the area: the corners, the middle and the sides.)	Is it easier or harder to swerve and avoid each other in a large or small area?
Developing skills and their application through Memory Trail	• In advance, set out a string trail, ideally in a wooded area or along a semi-obscured fence. • Hang 20 random objects at intervals along the string, eg. key, scissors, whistle, CD, etc. (ideally have these attached to clothes pegs for ease of setting up). • The trail is marked with a string, which may go high or low and pass through or behind obstacles. • You must not touch the string or objects. • Split the class into groups of 5-6. • You will find unexpected objects along the trail; you must remember what you see. • The trail is not a race. Do not overtake the group in front. • At the end, in a group, write down all the objects that you can remember. • Differentiate as appropriate.	How careful were you to follow the trail? When you spotted an object, did you keep quiet and not let other groups know about it? Had you planned sufficiently before you started?
Additional ideas	• Pupils carry clipboards and write down or draw the objects as they see them. • Hang letters from the cord. The letters could spell a word or message, either directly or as an anagram. • Hang objects or letters at random in a wild area with fixed boundaries, or around the outside of the school building. There is no need for a string; pupils must search the whole area. • Try a team search. Use cards with a number on each card eg: '2H'. Teams are given a coded number message and have to decipher the message. All teams can use the same area at the same time. Please feed back comments and additional ideas at www.caaps.org.uk	
Review and assess (Cool-down)	As a group, discuss the items you may have missed. Discuss other 'methods' for remembering items.	What was your favourite item that you found? If you were to do the activity again, what would you do differently?

Learning Outcomes:
Least able: Will be able to follow a simple trail being led by a partner or small group.
Majority: Will be able to follow a short trail and go from one place to another working cooperatively.
Most able: Will be proactive in organising the group to solve the challenge set.

Teacher's notes to inform future planning:

Teacher's notes to inform future planning:

LESSON 4 – MAP SYMBOL RACE

ACTIVITY:
Identifying map symbols and matching them with their correct names

LEARNING OBJECTIVE:
To reinforce learning

ORGANISATION AND RESOURCES:
Photocopied sets of 10-15 map symbols and corresponding names (see resources). 1 set per team of 4-5

YEAR 3

LESSON 4 – MAP SYMBOL RACE

LESSON PHASE	LEARNING ACTIVITY	PLANNED QUESTIONS
Starter activity (Warm-up)	• Jog, lifting knees high on the spot, and then on the move. • On command from the teacher, jog lifting knees higher and faster or jog slowly. • Alternate, fast and slow, fast and slow. Introduce the 'stop' command to check quick reaction times.	Can you move faster if you use your arms? What is the best arm action? Can you pump the air, with elbows driving back and fists clenched? How high can you get your knees? Can you keep going fast for 30 seconds; I minute? Can you stop quickly on the signal?
Developing skills and their application through Map Symbol Race	• Make 6 photocopies of both the map symbols and names (and ideally laminate these). • Guillotine the sheets where indicated and collate into 6 sets of symbols and 6 sets of names. • Each team of 4-6 has a set of cards. • Put the cards with map symbol names in a pack face down on one side of the playground (or field), in front of each team. • Spread the map symbols of each set, face up, on the other side of the playground, opposite each team. • Hold each map symbol up in turn and tell the class what it represents, eg. 'This is a road'. • This is a relay: the first runner in each team picks up the top name card, runs across the playground and picks up the corresponding 'symbol' card. • Then runs back to the start with both cards and lays them out on the ground, face up. • Next runner goes. • Repeat until all cards are matched. • Differentiate as appropriate.	Was each card matched correctly? Did your team remember all the symbols? What methods could you use to help remember the symbols?
Additional ideas	• Increase/decrease the numbers in the team. • Shorten/increase the running distance. • Do this as an individual activity. • Instead of map symbols, use question and answer cards based on what pupils have recently been learning. • Use jigsaw maps instead of sets of cards. The pieces are put on one side of the playground and a master copy on the other. Runners carry one piece at a time. • Have sets of laminated maps of the school site; one map with several features marked on it and the other map with none. Put the blank maps with a marker pen on the far side of the playground. Put the maps with features on in front of the teams. Using map memory, each runner has to run and copy a feature onto the blank map and return. Please feed back comments and additional ideas at www.caaps.org.uk	
Review and assess (Cool-down)	Discuss with the group the correct symbols and names. Return the cards to the correct piles by walking.	

Learning Outcomes:
Least able: Will be able to follow a simple trail being led by a partner or small group.
Majority: Will be able to follow a short trail and go from one place to another working cooperatively.
Most able: Will be proactive in organising the group to solve the challenge set.

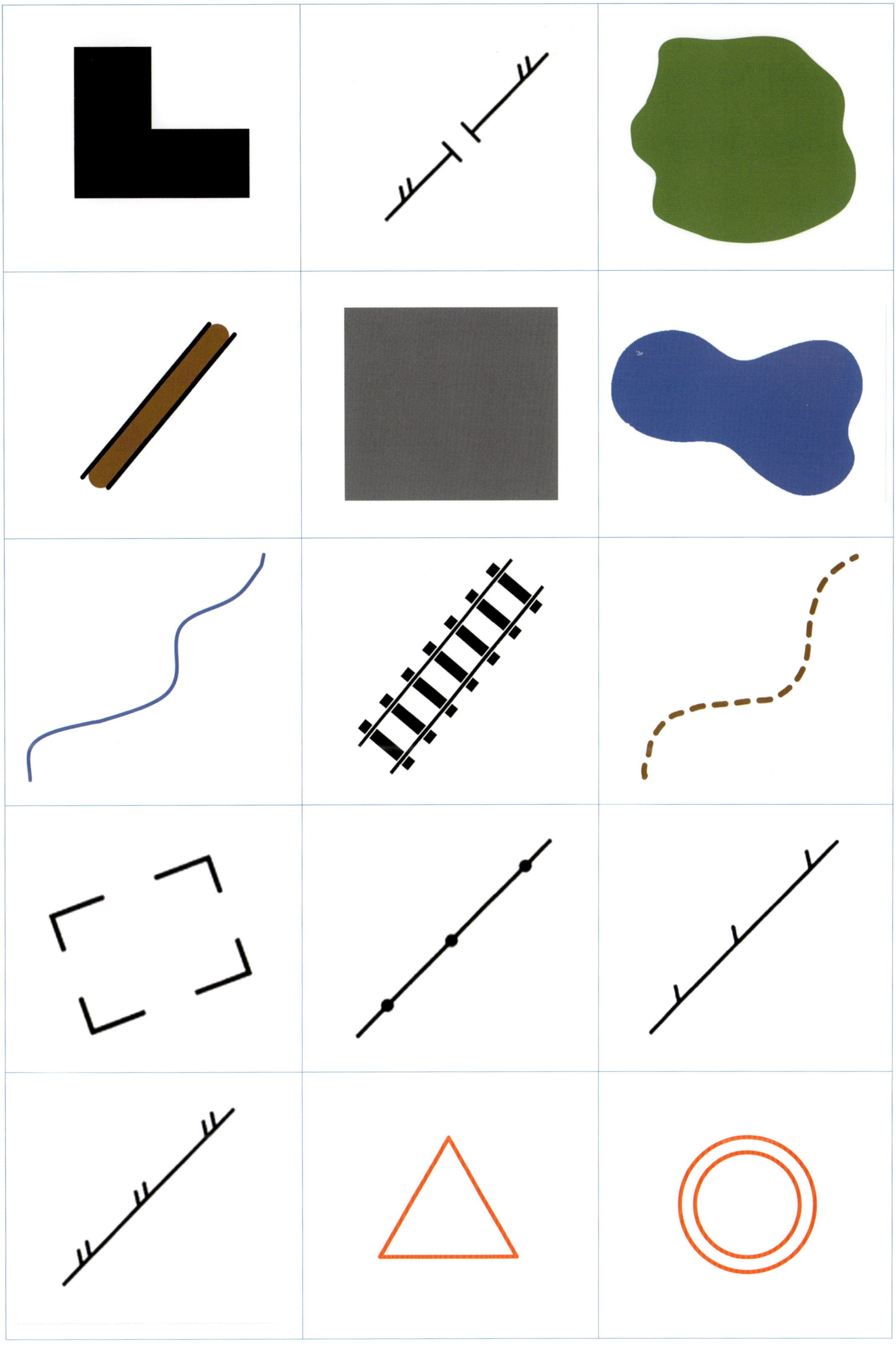

Building	Gate	Forest
Road	Tarmac	Lake
Stream	Railway	Track
Ruin	Wall	Low Fence
High Fence	Start	Finish

Teacher's notes to inform future planning:

Teacher's notes to inform future planning:

LESSON 5 – CLIPPING CONTROL CARDS

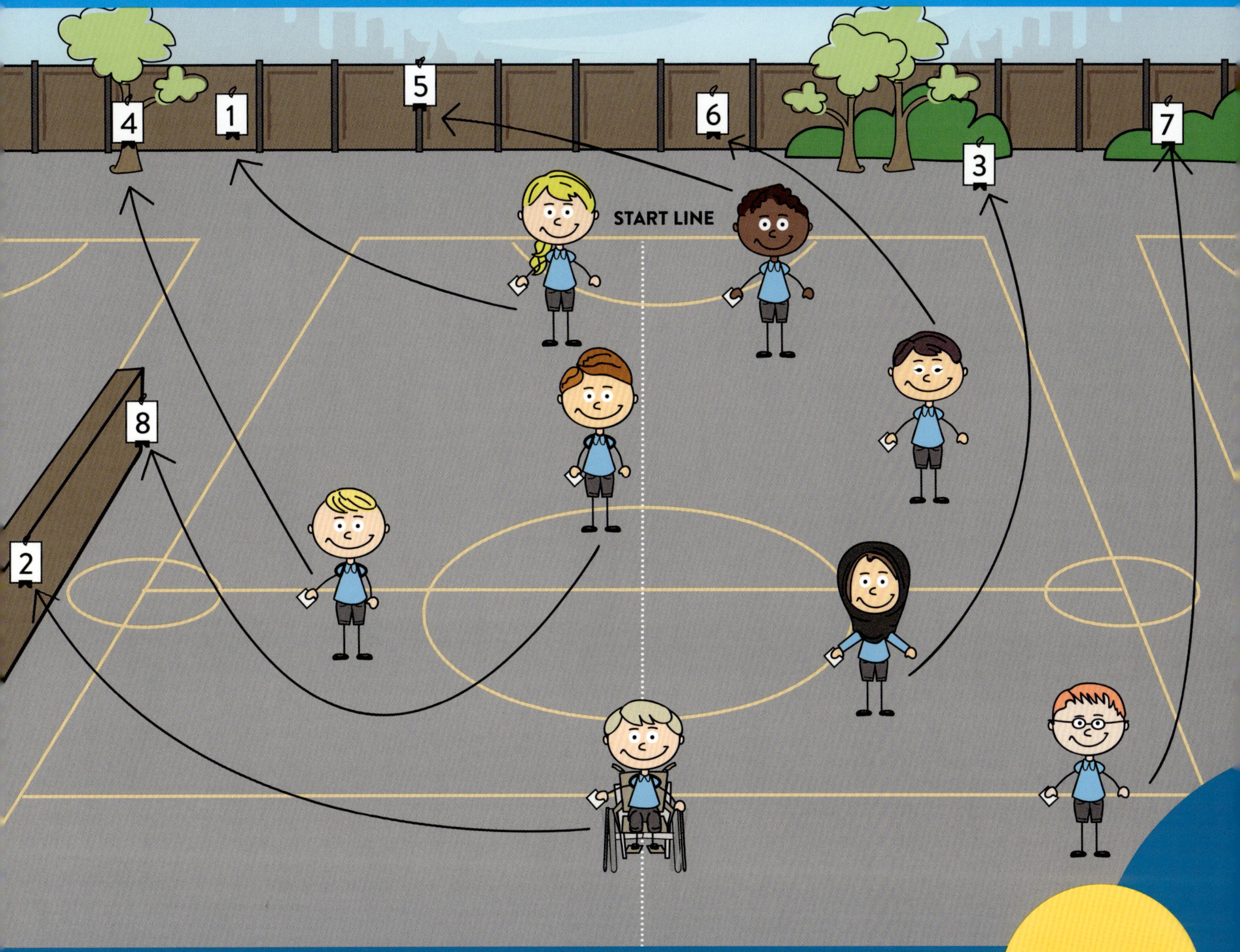

ACTIVITY:
Locating and 'clipping' (or otherwise marking) control cards as quickly as possible

LEARNING OBJECTIVE:
To communicate in a teamwork situation

ORGANISATION AND RESOURCES:
20 orienteering clippers (punches), or similar items, numbered 1-20 (see page 9). Photocopied 'control cards' (see resources)

YEAR 3

LESSON 5 – CLIPPING CONTROL CARDS

LESSON PHASE	LEARNING ACTIVITY	PLANNED QUESTIONS
Starter activity (Warm-up)	• Take a look around. Is the area we are using safe? • In pairs, jog behind each other like a car and a caravan. • On the command from the teacher, the caravan overtakes the car and takes the lead, jogging in any direction. • On the next command, the car jogs to the front and takes over the lead. • Join groups to make 4s and repeat the car and caravan game.	Is it easier to jog around the playing area, or jog in and out of everyone? Can you change direction whilst jogging in pairs, without stumbling or bumping into each other? What is happening to your heart as you jog faster? Does anyone know why it beats faster?
Developing skills and their application through Clipping Control Cards	• Hang all 20 clippers around the playground at random. • Split class into groups of 3. • Explain what a 'control card' is, and that they will be using different control cards for different activities until the end of Year 6. • Each group has a control card for marking (clipping) the answers. • This can either be a relay or group activity. • On 'go', pupils run to the clippers and mark the control card in the correct box (eg Clipper 12 in box 12). • Repeat until you have visited all 20 clippers. • Allow sufficient planning time. • Differentiate as appropriate.	What was your plan to get to all of the clippers as quickly as possible? How could you have completed this exercise more quickly?
Additional ideas	• Put the controls in number order, eg 2,4,6; 1,3,5 on opposite sides of playground. • Give teams scissors to cut the control card and distribute. • Make a set of large cards with orienteering signs and symbols on (eg start, finish, tree, fence, etc). Number the cards 1-12. Make an identical set but mark these with letters, A-L. Put the cards out on the field or playground, numbers on one side, letters on the other. Give each pupil a card and pencil stub/crayon. They have to match the numbered symbol cards to the lettered symbol cards. Please feed back comments and additional ideas at www.caaps.org.uk	
Review and assess (Cool-down)	Ask the pupils to walk to collect the clippers.	Describe how you were able to clip all 20 boxes on your control card? How could you improve your efficiency next time?

Learning Outcomes:
Least able: Will be able to describe what they did when solving the challenge.
Majority: Will be able to comment on how they went about tackling the challenge.
Most able: Will be able to explain reasons for choosing the approach used in the challenge and recognise other possible approaches.

NAMES:

1	2	3	4	5	6	7	8	9	10

11	12	13	14	15	16	17	18	19	20

NAMES:

1	2	3	4	5	6	7	8	9	10

11	12	13	14	15	16	17	18	19	20

NAMES:

1	2	3	4	5	6	7	8	9	10

11	12	13	14	15	16	17	18	19	20

Teacher's notes to inform future planning:

LESSON 6 – FOLLOW THE STRING

www.caaps.org.uk

ACTIVITY:
Following a string trail and writing down the hanging letters found on the way around

LEARNING OBJECTIVE:
To be able to solve a problem using ideas learned previously

ORGANISATION AND RESOURCES:
300m+ string or other cord. 10 hanging letters (ideally 1/4 A4 card with a letter on, A-J), laminated and attached to a clothes peg for ease of setting up. Blank paper. Pencil stubs/crayons. Maps (optional)

YEAR 3

LESSON 6 – FOLLOW THE STRING

LESSON PHASE	LEARNING ACTIVITY	PLANNED QUESTIONS
Starter activity (Warm-up)	• In pairs, shuttle running. Stand behind each other on the shorter line of a netball court (the shooting circle end). • On the whistle, the front person runs to the first line and back and then the next one goes. Then they run to the second line and back alternately. Lastly, they run all the way to the other end line and back, alternately.	How many shuttles can you do in 1 minute/2 minutes? (There and back equals one shuttle). What is happening to your body after you have been shuttle running at full speed?
Developing skills and their application through Follow The String	• This is a timed race to the finish. • Set up a string trail of 300m+ in a suitable area. Thin string or wool, which would break easily, is best for safety reasons. (It is more manageable if you keep the string in 50m reels, as ends do not need to be tied together). • Hang 10 cards with answer letters on at random intervals along the string. • This is a timed race to the finish. • Set each pupil/pair off on the course with a piece of paper and pencil stub/crayon at separate times. (Alternate pairs can go the other way round the course.) • They run to the letters along the course and write these down in the correct order. • Review the activity. • Repeat the activity. If using maps, repeat, marking the map with the location of each letter. • Give pupils responsibility for timing themselves. • Differentiate as appropriate.	What was your plan to get to all the letters as quickly as possible? Did you visit all the letters and mark them on your card?
Additional ideas	• To make it more challenging, attach a streamer or other marker to the string – this indicates that the clipper is not on the string, but somewhere nearby. Please feed back comments and additional ideas at www.caaps.org.uk	
Review and assess (Cool-down)	Ask the pupils to walk in groups to collect in the letters. Collect in the string.	How could you improve your efficiency next time?

Learning Outcomes:
Least able: Will help others to solve the problem taking an active part in the task.
Majority: Will be able to respond successfully to the problem set.
Most able: Will be able to use ideas learned previously to help solve the problem.

Teacher's notes to inform future planning:

Teacher's notes to inform future planning:

LESSON 7 – ROLLING BALL

ACTIVITY:
Teams must coordinate themselves in order to get the tennis ball from the start line to the finish line without dropping it

LEARNING OBJECTIVE:
To work cooperatively and safely in pairs and small groups

ORGANISATION AND RESOURCES:
16 short lengths of plastic guttering (see description).
5 tennis balls. 5 containers/boxes

YEAR 3

LESSON 7 – ROLLING BALL

LESSON PHASE	LEARNING ACTIVITY	PLANNED QUESTIONS
Starter activity (Warm-up)	• In pairs, shuttle running. • Stand behind each other on the side-line of a netball court, the front person runs to the opposite side line and back and then the next one goes. • Repeat for one minute and count how many shuttles take place. (There and back equals one shuffe).	Why do we need to warm up before a physical activity? Does shuttle running increase the heart rate more than jogging in and out of spaces on the pllayground? (Yes) Why is this?
Developing skills and their application through Rolling Ball	• In teams of 6-8. • This activity works best on a playground with line markings or chalked start/finish lines. • Obtain/cut 16 pieces of standard plastic half-pipe guttering (of random lengths between 60 and 100cms). • Each pair in the team has a section of guttering (half-pipe). • Each team has 1 tennis ball. • Mark out a start and finish line. This must be further than the total length of each team's half-pipes. • Put a container at the finish line opposite each team. • Teams must safely transfer their ball from the start to the end container. • The ball cannot be touched at any time, except when putting it into the first half-pipe. • When the ball is in a section of half-pipe, the people holding the half-pipe must not move. • Allow teams ample time to plan. • If the ball falls out then the team must start again. • Differentiate as appropriate.	Did you work well as a team? If you dropped the ball, why did this happen?
Additional ideas	• Include obstacles for the group to navigate over or under. • Vary the size and weight of the ball (large sponge balls are easier, golf balls are harder). • Set a time limit. • No talking after the planning phase. • Go there and back (ball remains in half-pipe throughout). • Allow practice attempts before the main attempt. Please feed back comments and additional ideas at www.caaps.org.uk	
Review and assess (Cool-down)	Discuss how you worked as a team and how you could improve on this next time.	What could you do next time to not drop the ball? What could you do next time to improve your speed?

Learning Outcomes:
Least able: Will be able to follow others' suggestions.
Majority: Will be able to work and behave safely with others.
Most able: Will be able to take a leadership role in solving the challenge.